Philip Gilbert Hamerton

The Unknown River

Philip Gilbert Hamerton

The Unknown River

ISBN/EAN: 9783744791052

Printed in Europe, USA, Canada, Australia, Japan

Cover: Foto ©ninafisch / pixelio.de

More available books at **www.hansebooks.com**

THE UNKNOWN RIVER.

AN ETCHER'S VOYAGE OF DISCOVERY.

With Thirty-seven Illustrations,

ETCHED FROM NATURE BY THE AUTHOR.

THE

UNKNOWN

BY

PHILIP GILBERT HAMERTON.

Illustrated by the Author.

BOSTON:
ROBERTS BROTHERS.
1872.

Press of
JOHN WILSON AND SON,
Cambridge.

TO

THE REV. HORATIO N. POWERS, D.D.,

RECTOR OF ST. JOHN'S, CHICAGO,

*One of the most valued of many kind friends
in America,*

I DEDICATE THIS VOLUME.

PREFACE

TO THE AMERICAN EDITION.

IN the revival of the too long neglected art of etching, we who in England and France have tried to recover the right use of the needle, have had to contend against many difficulties; and little of what we have hitherto done can be considered more than tentative and experimental. Etching, however, has this advantage over line-engraving, — that the comparatively rapid and spontaneous nature of the process, and its purely artistic and intellectual aims, obtain indulgence for many imperfections which would not be tolerated in a craft professing great mechanical finish. In etching, the spirit of the work is of more consequence than manual accuracy, and I have therefore allowed several plates to be published in this series, in which the manual work is rude, because they expressed my meaning, though in a rough way. Nearly all the plates in this series — indeed, the whole of the landscape subjects — were etched directly from nature, often under circumstances very different from the convenient surroundings of an engraver's table at home, with rain pouring over the plate, or daylight rapidly declining, joined to serious apprehensions about passing some dangerous rapid before I could get to a village inn, or find shelter beneath the thatch of some humble hamlet, nestled in a nook of the wooded and rocky shore. Hence they are literally no more than the notes of impressions which an artist takes in his memorandum book. As for the two or three subjects in which the author himself appears, it may be remarked that, as he could not *pose* and draw at the same time, there was a peculiar difficulty in these attempts, which the author, from want of practice in figure drawing, could scarcely be expected to overcome. A friend of mine, who is a figure-painter by profession, kindly made one or two slight sketches as helps; but, as the artist in question belonged to the severest French classical school (with which, as an artist, I have no affinity whatever, though as a critic I admire much of what it has accomplished), his sketches were conceived in a temper so opposed to mine that they turned out to be of no use for this particular purpose. Dog Tom was introduced at the urgent request of an unknown correspondent whose love of dogs touched the author in a tender place, and made him, somewhat rashly, turn animal-designer for the occasion. American critics are therefore requested to remember that the figures and dog are thrown in, as it were, simply for the reader's amusement, and not with any ambitious artistic pretensions.

However, such as they are, it has been the good fortune of these little plates to please many people in Europe, and amongst them a few more than ordinarily fastidious and capable judges. This may be attributed to the fact that in etching them the artist worked without the least reference to criticism of any kind, in the simple enjoyment of one of the pleasantest artistic expeditions imaginable. Indeed, although working very hard the whole time, I was under the delusion — it may be strictly said, *labored* under the delusion — that the voyage was a perfect holiday, a belief that was greatly encouraged by an absolute indecision as to which plates should be published and which destroyed. Another piece of luck was, that I had no time, nor acid, to bite the plates there and then, and so innocently fancied that they were all very pretty (an etching done according to the old negative process always looks pretty when it is first drawn, because the lines glitter charmingly on the black ground), and felt agreeably encouraged, the evil hour of disappointment being put off until my return to home and the printing press, which told the painful truth with a frankness equal to that of the most unpleasantly honest *dilettante* in England.

It may interest readers who share the author's boating propensities to know that the voyage was undertaken in a canoe fabricated by his own hands of paper, on a light skeleton of laths. The whole of the voyage was accomplished in this fragile craft; but it is only honest to add that she became leaky before it was over, and was condemned as unriverworthy at the end. Not that I think, even now, that paper is a bad material for canoes, but I had not then (1866) hit upon the right material for gluing it. I employed the *enduit Ruolz*, which takes about twelve months to harden, and I had not patience to wait the twelve months; so the sheets or bands of paper did not really adhere, and the water oozed between them after a while. The proper gum to use for fastening paper so as to resist water is simply a strong solution of shell-lac in spirits of wine. I have a canoe at present and two small punts which are made of thin wood, lined with paper, applied with shell-lac. When a leak shows itself it is stopped at once with a bit of paper and a touch of the solution, which dries immediately. An English oarsman tells me that for the last two years he has used bits of calico with the same solution in an old wooden canoe, which remains serviceable, thanks to the shell-lac. One result of the voyage narrated in this volume, was the invention of a machine which is a punt by day on the water, and a hut by night on shore, large enough to stretch a hammock in. The American reader will no doubt pardon an allusion to these fancies, and believe them compatible with serious work in other ways. If it is boyish to like boating, in all its forms (as some grave and wise men seem to imagine), I hope to remain puerile yet a little longer. The cold sapience of age comes on rapidly enough to all of us; and it is not a misfortune to be able still to feel an irrational delight in a canoe when she glides in safety, and an imprudent indifference when she upsets.

The verses at the beginning of this book were written during the late war, in anticipation of an attack from the Germans, which took place shortly afterwards; and I witnessed the combat for many hours on the banks of the river, between Garibaldi, who defended Autun, and a strong body of Bavarians who attacked it, — not exactly the moment for descending the river in a paper canoe! Another chapter was added that day to the long history of that ancient city by the Arroux; and as I watched the flight of the shells in the clear December air, and saw, beneath the moon, the fiery tongues darting from the mouths of the enemy's guns, I thought of many a former siege in times when war was less noisy and less bloody, but more cruelly protracted. How little I imagined, when writing the chapter about Augustodunum in this book, that I should see an army in battle array drawn up against it,—a dark, thick line of Germans with cannon glittering at intervals! Yet once again the Roman wall rang in echoes to the war-trumpet, and once again the river was stained with blood!

LIST OF ILLUSTRATIONS.

	PAGE
THE GATE-TOWER AT CHASEUX	*Title.*
ON THE TERNIN	1
PRE CHARMOY	2
MILLERY	5
VOUDENAY-LE-CHATEAU	8
DANGER AHEAD	11
NEAR VOUDENAY	12
A DIFFICULT PLACE	13
CROSSING A FIELD	15
CHATEAU OF IGORNAY	17
CATHEDRAL AND BISHOP'S PALACE, AUTUN	19
TOWERS OF AUTUN	21
GENETOIE	23
NEAR ORNAY	26
CASTLE OF CHASEUX	28
THE MOAT OF CHASEUX	29
TWILIGHT ON THE RIVER	30
OLD HOUSES AT ETANG	31
BETWEEN ETANG AND ST. NISIER	35
GREAT OAK OF ST. NISIER	36
MILL AT ST. NISIER	38
ROCKS AT ST. NISIER	41
BLOST	43

xiv *List of Illustrations.*

	PAGE
BETWEEN BLOST AND LABOULAYE	44
LABOULAYE	46
ROCK IN MIDSTREAM	50
RECUANGE I.	51
RECUANGE II.	53
TOULON-SUR-ARROUX	54
THE BRIDGE OF TOULON	55
ROCHE MALADROITE	58
GUEUGNON	61
SEEKING SHELTER	63
A NIGHT IN THE CANOE	64
PORTRAIT OF TOM	66
BRIDGE OF DIGOIN	68
RIVER SHORE NEAR DIGOIN	69

The wild rain drives in gusty showers,
  And past the moon the storm-clouds fly.
  The river, rising, hurries by
The gray 'old city of fair towers.'

The bayonets gleam in all her streets:
  All hearts are anxious, homes are sad—
  Oh, when shall victory make them glad,
And light the faces that one meets?

O River! once so fair and clear,
  Now dark as death thy currents flow;
  They may be reddened—who can know?—
Before the closing of the year.

O River! made for my delight,
  I see upon thy wintry flood
  A floating corpse—a streak of blood,
And flames reflected in the night!

October, 1870.

THE UNKNOWN RIVER.

CHAPTER I.

ON a bright afternoon in autumn I lay on the green bank of a little stream. The stream was so little that my dog Tom cleared it at one bound, as in the eager excitement of a wildly impossible chase he rushed after flying game. Of course he never yet caught a bird on the wing, but his faith in the practicability of such an achievement does not seem to be in the least shaken by the discouraging lessons of a constantly recurring experience. Only a peregrine falcon, strong-winged, sharp-taloned, could follow and slay those partridges, but Tom dashes after them through and over all manner of obstacles, hoping, by perseverance, to attain his object, like the man who ran after the express train.

Tom is a dog of immense energy when out of doors, and the most listless indolence at home. He will run a hundred miles in a day, or swim fifteen, but he will not walk across the room without the most elaborate preparation in the way of stretchings which he believes to be necessary, and when the little distance is at last accomplished he falls down with a grunt as if extenuated by fatigue. Another peculiarity of his is the wonderful difference in the state of his affections, for when in the open air he is in the highest degree grateful for the least word or gesture of his master, and very demonstrative himself, whereas in the studio, where he passes too many tedious hours, he has scarcely ever been known to acknowledge a caress even by one movement of his tail. He is by race a setter, and seemed destined to a sporting career, but, as his master's fowling-piece has not been used for some years, Tom's instincts are quite undisciplined, and though in outward appearance the finest setter in the whole neighborhood, so that all sportsmen stop and look at him when he passes by, he is a lamentable instance of the consequences of a neglected education, and almost any dog of the same breed is professionally his superior, if only he has passed through a proper course of discipline.

We digressed into this talk about Tom after saying that he jumped over a brook. The brook murmurs over the pebbles about a hundred yards lower down, and we hear the refreshing sound coming on the faint, cool breeze; but the brook is very calm and quiet just here, and washes its sandy banks with silent regularity, taking the earth away grain by grain, an unceasing agent of waste, and author of endless change.

There is no rest to faculties wearied by labor like rest by a quiet stream, on a beautiful afternoon in summer. If you distribute your work wisely, and are fortunate enough to have work of a kind that may be done at your own hours, you will take care, when the days are long, to reserve some considerable part of the afternoon as sacred to utter idleness, and if a quiet stream is within an easy distance, there will you go and rest. Most men under such circumstances take a rod and fish, but it does not always happen that there is any thing which the dignity of manhood may avow an interest in catching. The

man who rents a salmon river in Scotland, or even the Englishman whose trout stream is well preserved, may go forth with the implements of the angler and a consciousness of noble aims. But can anybody past boyhood pretend to take an interest in catching minnows, unless, indeed, he be a Frenchman who has just landed a *goujon*, and is vain of the exploit?

It is curious how capable we all are of seeing people and things every day of our lives without being once prompted to ascertain any thing further about them,— whence they come, whither they go, what their past has been, or what may be reserved for them in the future. The inhabitants of great cities, being satiated by the continual sight of innumerable persons and things, have this indifference in the most strongly developed form, but it may be observed in the country with regard to what is most commonly seen there. For instance, brooks and streams are very commonly met with in all northern countries, and therefore very few people ever give a thought to the geography of them, or have any thing beyond a very vague and general notion of their course. The inhabitants of the region through which the stream passes usually know it at bridges and fords, and farmers know it where it eats away the land, and where, in times of flood, it is most likely to leave a deposit of sand and pebbles; the angler, too, may have followed it for a few miles, and some professional landscape-painter or amateur may have explored a few of its most picturesque parts. But no man living knows the whole stream, and so there is always a great mystery about it, and any one who cares to follow its course faithfully may enjoy all the keen delights, and feel all the unceasing interest, which belong to a true exploration.

In this especial sense our little river is indeed unknown, and as I lay idly on its bank on that bright autumn afternoon, it occurred to me clearly for the first time that the river came from far, and went yet farther, that it was not confined to the fields about my house, and that this little scene was not a solitary gem, but one only of a thousand links in a long chain of various and unimagined beauty.

Why had not this been equally clear to me years before? Why do we dream ever in one place, or travel by the same weary old roads, when infinite beauty and novelty are open to us? It is because the beauty and the novelty are so *very* near to us that we miss them, and often so cheap that our pitiful small dignity despises them as something puerile. When we are weary of the monotony of life, and the whole human organism longs for the refreshment of change, we would go to the end of the earth, and in order to defeat our purposes as completely as possible, carry our habits with us. We are accustomed to railways and newspapers, to bitter ale and sweet tea, and we seek these things, and a thousand others that habit has rendered necessary, wherever on earth we go. And yet change more refreshing, and novelty more complete are here within one day of slowest travel, than in journeys to Berlin and Vienna, for the truest change and best novelty are not in length of travel, but in the abandonment of habit, and especially in the zest of free and personal discovery.

There is an unfortunate belief that this glorious pleasure and passion of the discoverer are not now to be enjoyed in Europe. It is supposed that since every State in that region has been explored by many travellers, and even more or less accurately surveyed by the makers of maps, there is nothing new to be found there. The rea-

An Etcher's Voyage of Discovery. 5

son for this appears to be a confusion between the genuine pleasures of the discoverer and the satisfaction of his pride. Of course there can be nothing to boast of in discoveries such as those here narrated, but there is much to be enjoyed. The explorer of a nameless European river need not hope to be remembered like Livingstone or Speke, but he may set forth in the full assurance of finding much that is worth finding, and of enjoying many of the sensations, deducting those connected with personal vanity, which give interest to more famous explorations. It is necessary, however, to the complete enjoyment of an excursion of discovery, that the region to be explored, whether mountain or river, or whatever else it may be, should not have been already explored by others, or at any rate not with the same objects and intentions. A geologist has a certain satisfaction in marching, hammer in hand, over a tract of country not yet conquered for geology; and an artist likes to sketch in secluded valleys where it is not probable that any artist has been before. On the same principle a traveller who is fond of boating has an especial pleasure in descending some stream of which it may be safely presumed that nobody ever descended it in a boat. In this especial sense there is much yet to be done in the way of exploration, even in the most known countries.

No sooner had these ideas formed themselves in the writer's mind, than the little stream by which he was lazily reclining acquired a new importance, and the low music of its shallows, instead of being, as formerly, the lullaby of Mother Nature, became an awakening call to action, and a promise of joyful change. A thousand scenes rose rapidly before his mind, and the pipe which had languidly yielded half an hour before the tiniest puffs of smoke to the fragrant air now gave dense clouds, in which the smoker saw endless visions. He saw the deep, calm pools under the rich overhanging foliage where the currents fall asleep together, like tired children that have filled the fields with their merry noise, till weariness fell on their swift limbs, and hushed their happy voices, and laid them in silent sleep under the soft green leaves. He saw the rapids dashing into white foam amongst the rocks, and the kingfisher glancing above them like a sapphire-flash in the sun. He saw the picturesque farms and cottages by the unfrequented shore, the gray, deserted castles, the antique cities, — the remains of a thousand years. And then came the majesty of the effects of nature, the splendor of the sunset and the promise of the dawn, the mysterious poetry of summer twilight and the long hours alone beneath the moon.

By this time it became impossible to remain quiet in that place any longer. Tom was called back from his vagrant courses and taken into his master's confidence. Tom listened with the utmost attention whilst the novel project was explained to him, and, although he may not have clearly understood its details, he perceived at least that action of some kind was meditated, and eagerly expressed his willingness to take a share in it.

CHAPTER II.

DURING the last few years the noble old art of etching has been revived by many painters. Some of my friends have practised it with distinguished success, and their example led me to recur to an art which I had first attempted in boyhood, and then neglected for many years. Of the means at my disposal for the illustration of the projected voyage none seemed better than etching, as it is the only kind of engraving which can be done directly from nature, and the only engraving, too, which has enough of the spirit of liberty to harmonize with such a state of mind as that of a wandering canoist. It accepts laborious finish when the artist has time for it, but it also allows of rapid sketching when he is in a hurry. So it was decided that the voyage should be written, and that the illustrations should be etched from nature on the way.

All the plates being prepared at home in my own etching-room (nearly sixty of them), I laid them on small drawing-boards, four to each board, and, by means of two very small screws to each plate, fixed them to the board so as to resist any jolting that they might be exposed to. There was no necessity to pierce the plates with holes to receive the screws, since, by placing the screws near the edge of the copper, the screw-heads held the plates firmly enough. I had previously tried many experiments for the carriage of plates, but none succeeded so well as this. If the coppers had been all of *precisely* the same dimensions, they might have been carried in a grooved box, such as photographers use for their glasses; and this, no doubt, would have been a considerable economy of space, and would, at the same time, have saved the weight of all drawing-boards except one.*

Having screwed my sixty plates to a quantity of small drawing-boards, I slipped these boards into several grooved boxes; each box provided with a lock and key. I then calculated the probable length of the voyage, and, having locked my boxes, sent them to inns at different distances down the river, to await my arrival. Thus I was never obliged to carry more than one box of plates at a time. It is unnecessary to go into the detail of my other preparations, which were of the kind now so well known to canoe-men, and to all who take an interest in canoe-travelling.

Here is the little village from which the expedition started. The canoe had been transported thither in a cart, and as we arrived in the evening it was not considered advisable to begin the voyage till the following day. So I dined at the little inn, and after dinner went out to walk in the village by the shore of the narrow rivulet I was to embark upon on the morrow.

It was a clear, bright moonlight night (the etching, it may be well to observe, is intended to represent a moonlight), and I wandered first about the river, and then in a small valley between precipitous little hills. I was in

---

* It is necessary, however, when plates are carried in a grooved box, without being fixed to a drawing-board, to revarnish their edges before biting.

the heart of the Morvan, a highland district in the east of France, almost unknown to tourists. The river to be explored was the Arroux, that passes by the antique Augustodunum, and flows to the historic Loire. Nobody had explored it yet, and all the hazards of the enterprise rose before me as I leaned over the low parapet of the one-arched bridge at Voudenay.

The stream flowed under the bridge, after a curve like a snake in the grass, a silvery snake glittering under the moon. It came from a rustic mill, and the monotonous noise of the mill-wheel was the only audible sound, except the wash of the swift current on its pebbly margin. Beyond the bridge the stream looked dark and treacherous (for the moon was behind me then), and it went and buried itself in a black wood. This was all that could be seen of it from Voudenay. It was very narrow, and wilful and swift, and it hurried away into the black wood as if it had some deadly unavowable work to do there, somebody to stifle and drown in the awful shade of the forest.

What would this adventure bring me to? No man knew the river, no man had ever known it. Its course was full of dangers. A thousand strong boughs were waiting for me, stretching their gnarled and knotty arms across the stream. There were festoons of briers and thorns, there were deep black pools hidden under the intricate branches, there were roots in the river, and lower down I had to expect sharp rocks also. But could I not swim? Yes, in *water*, but not amongst stones and snags. Better the angry waves of the ocean, than these treacherous suffocating snares!

There was just so much of apprehension as sufficed to give interest to the adventure. It amounted to a certainty that I should be upset (probably more than once), and have to struggle for dear life, but it was not so certain that I should struggle for it unsuccessfully. I returned to the little inn, and had a long talk with a set of peasants, and then went to bed in a room that looked out upon the river, the moonlight falling on the counterpane. The night was exquisitely calm, the peasants left the inn, and all the house was still.

I have accustomed myself to do with what suffices for the peasantry, and can therefore lodge in the poorest country inn or cottage without any painful sense of privation. This is a valuable accomplishment for an explorer of unknown rivers, who may have to lodge very simply from time to time. Thus, my first night I slept in the same room with a farmer's boy, my second with a wheelwright, and my third with the family of a poor miller; but I always had a bed to myself and clean sheets (though coarse). A sleepy traveller needs no more.*

We are afloat at last on the little river, which loses its terrors in broad daylight. I am in the paper canoe, and Tom is swimming behind. If that is the way he intends to follow me during the whole voyage he will incur much useless fatigue. Why does not Tom simply run along the bank? he would go twice as fast, with a tenth of the fatigue. I stop the canoe and reason with poor Tom. I explain all this to him both verbally and by signs, but his only answer is to look at me imploringly, and lift up his wet old nose, and splash with his fore-paws, and put one of them timidly on the edge of the canoe. I remove the paw, and use one word of menace: the sensitive

* I much prefer the independence of a tent, but in this voyage it did not seem practicable to carry a tent and provisions.

creature takes an expression of extreme sadness; I have wounded his feelings. I speak more kindly, and explain that the only objection is to his bigness; that he is dearly beloved, but unhappily too big; and that the canoe can never carry both of us. The kind tones encourage him again; this time he puts both paws on the canoe, and is within a hairbreadth of upsetting her. My only chance of getting the great, heavy, clinging paws off, is to hit their owner a smart rap on the nose with the paddle.

The narrow stream winds rapidly between banks of gravel, and four little boys are running along the shore, keeping pace with the swift canoe. Poor Tom cannot swim quite so fast, and has been left behind for several turns of the river, but now he comes galloping like a racehorse across the fields. Nothing could be easier and more agreeable than the voyage has hitherto been, but the stream, already very rapid, runs faster and faster, and is evidently carrying me into a dense grove of trees, which will probably be long, and which may offer very serious difficulties. The worst of these very narrow rivers is that there is not room to use the paddle, and you are carried along by the impetuous current with a very slight chance either of stopping yourself, if rushing upon obvious peril, or of defending yourself against the branches.

Here we are amongst the willows, carried rapidly down a little sylvan tunnel, three or four feet wide and about a yard high. It is wonderfully beautiful, if one had only the time to appreciate its beauty; but the current is so strong and impetuous, and the turns are so numerous, that there is hardly time to think of any thing but the management of the canoe. The little boys are behind somewhere, I hear their loud chatter in the distance, and a yelping bark from Tom informs me that he is yet alive, though I know not whether in water or on land.

The first insurmountable obstacle is a young tree, lying quite across the stream. It has not been cut down, but the water has eaten away the earth about its roots, and it has fallen across the current. If the place had been a little more open I might have hauled the canoe on shore and launched her a little lower down, but here the dense underwood makes that manœuvre impossible. Here come the little boys! I have a long and strong cord in the canoe; I tie a stone to one end of it, and throw it over a branch to a boy on the other side, telling him to tie it to the top of the fallen tree. Then, with the branch for a fulcrum, I and the little boys on my side pull very hard, and gradually the little tree rises and rises till the course is clear. After overcoming other difficulties with the help of the little boys, who were exceedingly useful, I came to a place where the river was less impetuous, and where I had leisure to admire its beauty. The canoe was floating pleasantly through a rich wood of oak and chestnut with here and there a group of graceful poplars. It was a constant succession of scenes like the one given opposite, whose exquisite loveliness it is not easy to convey by Art.

CHAPTER III.

THE etching which illustrated the end of our last chapter was done on the copper from nature at a little place that seemed convenient for lunch. A few square yards of firm sand-bank lay between the dense underwood and a deep pool, and this sand-bank was covered with short grass. The canoe was drawn up here, and her owner took out the materials for luncheon, and made what would have been a solitary meal, if Tom had not come up in great glee, doubly delighted at finding his master on *terra firma*, and all the signs of a festival spread out around him. Tom loves his master dearly, but his affection for beef and mutton is at least equally strong, and it is probable that the happiest hours of Tom's existence are such hours as this, when, in addition to the excitement of travel, and the free expenditure of his immense energy, he has the satisfaction of dining with his master on terms of something like equality. All the little boys had now been left behind except one, and he, unfortunately for his own interest, was on the other side of the stream. I wanted to get him over and invite him to lunch, and crossed for the purpose in the canoe; but the canoe only held one person, and the youth did not sit steadily, so that before we were two yards from the shore a capsize seemed inevitable, and I put back. After luncheon the voyage was resumed; the nature of it will be best gathered from the etching.

There are two little villages in the region where I was now voyaging, about a mile apart, and bearing the same name of Voudenay, so, to know one from the other, the inhabitants have called them Voudenay-l'Eglise and Voudenay-le-Château. My first day's voyage was from one of these villages to the other, total distance *one mile*. The reader may laugh if he likes, but that is about the proper degree of speed for an artist on his travels.

After dark, as I wished to get a few miles lower down the stream, I determined, as the moon did not rise till rather late, to continue the voyage by lamp-light. The canoe was provided with a carriage-lamp for the purpose, which was fixed in the forepart of the deck, and it was found quite possible to pursue a very intricate and sometimes even perilous navigation by the help of this artificial light. Where the narrow river was most thickly shaded on both sides by dense vegetation, the branches meeting immediately overhead, and festooned with overhanging creepers, the lamp-light gave a strange beauty to the scene; and as the canoe floated somewhat rapidly down this little green corridor, it seemed like a voyage in fairyland. Every tiny leaf and spray, every slender thread of stalk, came for one moment out of the blackness of night into the full brilliance of the lamp-light, then passed into the darkness behind. An endless succession of this inexhaustible loveliness made the night voyage one continual enchantment, and I was not sorry to have seen a river under an aspect so strikingly new. There exists, unfortunately, an especial difficulty in rendering the peculiar beauty of these effects in etching, and, knowing this, I have not wasted time in the attempt. The art of etching cannot reserve white lines of sufficient

thinness and purity to give the effect of lamp-light on delicate sprays and grasses. The effect would be broadly given, and it would be possible enough to reserve white lines,* but not with the fineness necessary to do full justice to the kind of delicacy which, in subjects such as these, would become the particular aim of the artist. Nothing struck me so much, in this delightful little voyage with the lamp, as the exquisite tenuity of the smaller plants as they came out with tiny leaves and stems against the black void of night. This might be approximately interpreted in wood-engraving, which most naturally works in white lines, but not so well in other processes. It was found that this voyaging by night added considerably to the interest of the exploration, for the mystery of the unknown was still more strongly felt when all that lay before us was in absolute darkness, and only became suddenly illuminated as the lamp approached.

He who attempts the exploration of a river not reputed navigable, must be prepared for passages of such extreme difficulty that it may be necessary to remove his canoe altogether from the water, and drag her over the dry land. The morning after the voyage by lamp-light I had a good deal of such work, so much that at length I lost patience and hired a spring-cart in which both the vessel and her owner were transported by a fast-trotting horse to a place four kilometres lower down, whilst Tom galloped along the road with a sense of freedom much greater than any which he had enjoyed amongst the tangled vegetation of the river's bank.

* For example, in the first plate in this series ('Unknown River,' Chap. I.), some thin stems were reserved by an application of stopping-out varnish.

When the boat was launched again, the stream took quite a new character. Instead of flowing with a current of equal breadth, and almost equal rapidity, it now alternately slept in calm pools and rushed hurriedly over short pebbly shallows. It is difficult, in words, to convey any idea of the variety of these beautiful pools, except by simply saying that they are various. If there were eighty of them, or a hundred of them, or however many there may have been, there were just as many new and admirable pictures. The shallows, too (though in passing rapidly over them we had not time to think of much but the safety of the canoe), were by no means the least interesting portions of the voyage, especially when they turned mysterious corners, and opened out new glimpses down the stream. At length we came to a pool so very long and so very tranquil that it seemed as if it would never end. The canoe glided over its glassy surface for many a long minute, and just as the explorer rested on his paddle and the little vessel had gone forward alone so long that the impetus was dying gradually away, something unwonted was reflected in the smooth water, and instead of the accustomed intricacy of boughs and fluttering of innumerable leaves, the voyager saw great stones as of a feudal castle, and surely on the green shore there stood a great ruin!

Whoever wishes to enjoy the sight of some noble ruin should come upon it in this unpremeditated way. One half the delight of it is in the surprise. When you have been told at starting by a guide-book, that 'at three miles from your inn is such a castle, now ruinous but formerly belonging to the Counts of, &c.,' and read the description of it in detail, you will either be quietly pleased or provokingly disappointed, but you will never

remained. Soon, however, the stream narrowed again, and an impetuous current rushed under closely woven boughs, and between many awkward snags. Many a place seemed impassable, but the stream was too swift and too narrow to admit of any going back, and there was nothing for it but to shut one's eyes and dash at the branches with the paddle lying useless on the deck. Once the boat was jammed between a root and a tree where the stream was strongest, but I got through by pulling at the tree with both hands. As for landing, it was out of the question; *there was no land to be seen*, nothing but branches, — branches everywhere, overhead, before, behind, to the right and to the left, with an impetuous current under them, strong, swift, and deep. Then I heard a roar of water amongst rocks, and in an instant, turning a corner, found myself at the foot of a steep hill, thickly wooded as far as I could see; and where the water had eaten into the hill the rocks were bare, a long row of them, and there were stones in the stream, over which it boiled with white foam. However, there was paddle-room, and I was really far safer than five minutes before under the branches. Whilst happily congratulating myself on my escape from so many difficulties, I turned a sharp corner; a long branch lay athwart the stream from side to side, two feet above the water; the boat passed under it, but I could not diminish myself sufficiently to pass under it too, so was upset in an instant, and fell in head first.

CHAPTER IV.

THE shipwreck that ended the last chapter occurred just at sunset. After a night's rest in a poor cottage, the voyage was resumed in the brilliant light of a new and cloudless day.

The river was still most dangerous, slipping furtively and fast through the thickest underwood, turning sharply in unforeseen ways and places, like a panther in the dense jungle.

At last, after being hurried down a narrow channel, with about as much freedom of will as the train in an atmospheric tube, we came suddenly out upon a great open pool. This was the confluence of the Arroux and the Drée, and the Arroux had doubled his substance by this alliance.

Before it, he had been a wild young rivulet of the most imprudent and impetuous character; after it, he had times of leisure, and lived in visible dignity, an important occupier of land. Imagine a constant succession of large and beautiful pools linked together by rapid babbling shallows on which the canoe darted gaily and swiftly without grounding. The pools were deep, with sloping bottoms of the finest sand, perfect bathing-places every one, and every one a picture.

After many windings, one curve of the beautiful river disclosed a noble city, rising far off on the slope of a lofty hill, blue in the haze of the bright afternoon, with massive walls and many towers. It is old Augustodunum, once the sister of Rome and her rival, since then strong in the middle ages with all the picturesque strength of turret and battlement, now narrowed till within the vast enclosure of the Roman fortifications the market-gardener grows his vegetables, and the farmer ploughs his fields. Still by the quiet river the Roman wall stands rugged, rich branches hanging over it, heavy and full, and striving to reach the flowing water. And the Roman gate still augustly receives the traveller as he crosses the bridge over the Arroux, its gray arches and pilasters borne high over the mighty portals with a little statue of the Virgin between them, record of the faith of the middle ages, and a gas-lamp to prove that the modern time has come.

A great and wonderful Roman city, one of the noblest in the Roman world, stood here on the banks of the Arroux. In the circuit of her walls were more than two hundred towers. She had a great amphitheatre, and innumerable temples, and theatres, and baths. The soil to this day is full of fragments of precious marbles from the luxurious Roman dwellings. For a thousand years the earth has been yielding a harvest of antiquities, still inexhaustible; columns, and statues, and bronzes, and pavements of Roman mosaic. And when the glorious Roman city, SOROR ET AEMULA ROMAE, was utterly ravaged and destroyed, there arose upon her site a mediæval city, smaller, yet not less beautiful, so that a king of France called it his 'City of Beautiful Towers.' But the mediæval city has disappeared almost as completely as the Roman. The classic amphitheatre is razed to the ground; of the mediæval cathedral (a great edifice of the purest Gothic) there remains *one* arch in a

An Etcher's Voyage of Discovery.   21

garden. The present cathedral is a church which stood under the shadow of the old one. A few fragments of the mediæval city remain here and there, the house of Rolin, chancellor of Burgundy, now a carpenter's shop, a tower of the old Donjon, and here and there a few houses of the thirteenth or fourteenth century. Still Autun is a picturesque and quaint place, full of endless subjects for an etcher.

If there is any thing in the history of the past that can move or interest the present, the past of this strange city cannot leave us cold. Who could float here on the Arroux, close to the Roman wall, without thinking of all that has happened here, by the shore of this now peaceful river? A simple catalogue of the vicissitudes of this city, unparalleled in the succession of her misfortunes, reads like some marvellous poem. The story of all her sieges has a Homeric grandeur.

First she was ravaged by Tetricus. After a resistance of seven months she was punished by the conqueror of Tetricus, Aurelian. Ruined by German hordes in the third century, she was sacked again under Diocletian. For twenty-five years she lay prostrate in her ashes, and the lands about her were untilled. She was punished again by Constantius after the defeat of Magnentius. She was besieged by Chonodomarus and Vestralphus; and after that by the Vandals; and after that by the Burgundians; and then by Attila, who massacred the inhabitants and reduced the whole place to ashes. Childebert and Clotaire ruined the city on the flight of Godmar. The Saracens sacked Autun; the Normans sacked it in 886, and a few years later Rollo pillaged it again. After the battle of Poictiers the English came and burnt part of the city. Admiral Coligny came and burnt a priory and the palace of an abbot, pillaging the abbey. Towards the end of the sixteenth century Autun was besieged by the Marshal Daumont, and her archives used for gun-wadding.

There are great incidents in her history: the martyrdom of St. Symphorien, the visit of Bishop Proculus to Attila. The reader may remember the great picture by Ingres, of the young Symphorien led by the Roman lictors to execution, his mother encouraging him from the wall. And if Symphorien sacrificed himself for his faith, Proculus did the same for his fellow-citizens. He went to Attila's camp to entreat him to spare the city, and Attila beheaded him.

A memorable circumstance, in another way, was the visit of Constantine to Autun. Constantine had raised the city from ruin and despair; rebuilt her edifices, re-established her schools. Finally he came in person with his court. The expression of the people's gratitude moved him to tears. He forgave them five whole years of taxes.

The saddest history connected with the city is that of poor Queen Brunehault, early in the seventh century. She wished to place her grandson (she had four) on the throne of her son Tyherri, who was dead. Clotaire II. had the four sons arrested. The queen herself was arrested near the lake of Yverdun, and taken to Clotaire's camp in Burgundy. Three days of torture ended by a derisive promenade on a camel through the camp. Her grandsons were slaughtered before her eyes; then she herself was tied to the tail of a wild horse. Her body was brought to Autun and laid in a marble tomb.

But the grandest and noblest action of all that shed lustre on the antique city, is the refusal of the Count de

An Etcher's Voyage of Discovery. 23

Charni to execute the massacre of St. Bartholomew. There were eight hundred Calvinists in the place, and the order came to slay them; but the advocate Jeannin recommended the *Bailly*, de Charni, to disobey the royal mandate, and they spared the Calvinists, to their own eternal honor. In his disobedience De Charni had the boldness to tell the king that he wished to leave him time to reflect upon orders issued in anger; and the Chancellor, on reading De Charni's letter to his majesty, observed, — '*C'est un juge de village qui nous prescrit notre devoir!*'

The bishops of Autun, when newly appointed, used to make a solemn entry into their city. They had an episcopal residence at Lucenay (an exquisitely beautiful little place amongst the hills), and the new bishop left this residence in state. But he did not enter Autun at once. First he stopped at the monastery of St. Andoche, without the walls, and the abbess was obliged to entertain him and all his retinue. Near the convent there was a country-house called Genetoie, and the proprietor of it was obliged to give the bishop hot water for his feet, an obligation much less heavy than that which fell upon the abbess. The bishop went to Genetoie to await the arrival of the chapter. When they came he presented himself at the closed door of the cloister, and was refused admission twice, answering each time that he was the bishop of Autun. The third time he was admitted, and took the oath.

The accompanying illustration shows all that remain of the house of Genetoie as it appeared when islanded by the flood of 1866.

CHAPTER V.

THE bishops made their entry into the city by the bridge of St. Andoche, but one of them went out of it again by the other bridge, and his carriage-wheels rattled on the road to Paris, and in Paris he took up a new trade which he practised with the most distinguished success. Can you fancy Talleyrand as a bishop, going about gravely in violet, and giving his precious benediction? All the portraits I ever saw of him represent him in court dress, and nothing is more difficult than to rid one's self, even temporarily, of an association. The converse difficulty is that of imagining Pius IX. as an officer of dragoons. Had it been possible to see the two together, in the garb of their first professions, who would have guessed which was to become a famous pope and which an equally celebrated diplomatist?

When Autun was left behind, the river went for half a mile in such a stately manner that anybody would have given it credit for being navigable in the most serious sense of the word, — navigable for vessels laden with much more valuable merchandise than the materials of an unpopular art. In this long, quiet reach the lads from the college came to practise themselves in swimming, and this led me to think about three youths who may have bathed here not so very long ago, but whose history was at least as romantic as that of the

Greek and Roman heroes they read about in their textbooks at the college. One of these youths was called Neapoleonne de Bounaparte,* and the two others were brothers of his. Napoleon did not remain quite four months at the college of Autun (the fact is unknown to all his biographers), but his brother Joseph stayed here as many years. Napoleon's little cell (the colleges had cells in those days) still existed two or three years since. It was positively known to be one of the five or six that remained, but which there was no means of ascertaining.

At length the towers of Autun, which showed themselves in glimpses during the windings of the river, and completed in this way a hundred pretty compositions, disappeared finally behind a spur of hill clothed with a dense pine-forest. Once more the canoe floated on a quite lonely river without evidence of human labor or habitation, except now and then the smoke of a distant farm, or the cry of the drivers of oxen, generally the name of each animal, sung out with a musical cadence. It was pleasant to get into the perfect country again, though Autun scarcely seems a city, and the Arroux flows past it undisturbed by human interference, except when the strong brown-skinned horsemen ride up to their waists in the water, and the fishermen cast their nets.

Westwards rose the blue mass of the Beuvray, where recent investigations have fixed the site of a city older than Augustodunum, the Bibracte of the Gauls. But Bibracte is almost without a history. Cæsar went there, and said that it was a great stronghold, and took provisions from it for his army, but left us scarcely a word of

* So entered on the college books.

description. Bibracte can never have been more than a great fortified hill-village, or Gaulish *oppidum*, composed of very rude huts, huddled close together, and protected by solid walls built in the strong Gaulish way, with logs nailed together with huge nails, and earth and stone between them. Floating down the river in the evening I saw the last flames of sunset die behind the Beuvray, and the majesty of its purple crests was enhanced by its ancient strength. What is on the hill-crest now? On the site of the buried city is a forest of old gnarled beeches, and in the midst of the forest stands a little camp of huts, where an antiquary passes his summers, with a band of faithful men. Even now, I thought, in the evening, he is standing on some brow of rock, and looking over the boundless plains. He can see the lands beyond the Loire, and the whole course of the river that I am obscurely exploring. And when the twilight comes, and his evening walk is over, he will go to his wooden hut and sleep amidst his trophies. A pleasant, enthusiastic, absorbed life he has of it up there! He tells me that there is danger in the delight of it, the danger of a too complete abandonment to the enjoyment of glorious nature and the dear antiquarian dream. He has a charming house in the city, with its *salons* filled with pictures and its museum with antiquities, and only a rough hut up there on the mountain; but every year as the summer comes he longs for the little hut, and the free range of the wild forest, and the fresh, high air, and the silence and the calm, and the healthy days of toil, and the lonely evening walks about the hill, and the vast, illimitable horizons. Whoever has once known this passion for wild nature, never, whilst health lasts, can lose it. There comes upon him

every year, first a vague uneasiness, then a craving and longing for something, he knows not what, and then he begins to dream at night of regions beautiful and wild. The streets of the town, even the spacious country-house, begin to feel like prisons, and he wants to get out into the forest, or on the mountain, or float on flowing rivers and tossing seas.

In consequence of having etched the little plate which the reader has just seen, I had to paddle some miles after sunset, and did not reach the next village until darkness had fairly set in. The river, fortunately, presented few of those dangers which had been so frequent in the earlier part of its course. There were a few rapids here and there, but not dangerous rapids, and now and then one of those disturbed places called '*remous*,' produced by sudden alterations in the form of the river's bed, often at a considerable depth. On the whole, however, the river was safer here than anywhere else on its whole course until it reached the plain of the Loire, and this will be readily understood after a few words on the geology of the district. The basin of Autun is a wide valley hollowed in the rock, formerly a lake-bed, and afterwards filled to the brim with alluvial deposits. It is through these deposits that the river cuts its serpentine course, and so long as it has to do with nothing but soft loam, and sand, and little rounded pebbles, the navigation is safe and easy. But when we come to the thick granite *lip* of the great basin, we shall find that the stream suddenly takes a new character. It is a lowland river in the basin of Autun, a highland stream for twenty miles as it crosses the rocky edge of the basin, and after that a lowland river again as it meanders through the plain of the Loire. This accounts for my getting safely to the inn after dark; a little lower down all night-travelling was out of the question.

But at the inn there was not a bed to be had, so I went to a country-house on the other side of the river, belonging to a rich land-owner whom I did not know personally, but who had an encouraging reputation for hospitality. Going to beg a night's lodging at a private house where you are unknown requires more assurance, I think, than any thing I ever attempted.

The master of the mansion was absent. The butler put his head out of a bedroom window and heard my petition. The butler was a very decent fellow; he dressed himself, and came downstairs, and kindly heard all I had to say. For a moment I believed the difficulty overcome, but unluckily the favorable impression which I had succeeded in making on this man's mind availed me nothing, for the supreme authority was the housekeeper. She put her face out of a window, an ugly visage whose thousand wrinkles were strongly illumined by a candle in her skinny hand, and one glance assured me that she would be inexorable. Nothing could be more decided than her refusal. And they talk of the tender-heartedness of women!

How and where I passed that night shall be a mystery. How do vagrants and vagabonds pass theirs?

This castle is the Castle of Chaseux, a picturesque old ruin by the river-side, in a charming situation. The effect is more picturesque in the etching than in the reality, because he who only sees the drawing does not realize the curiously small scale of the towers. They are decidedly the tiniest towers I ever saw in any castle of feudal times; but they looked larger, no doubt, when they had their pepper-box roofs. For the rest the place

is not without grandeur, and it has some literary interest as an occasional residence of Madame de Sévigné with that cousin of hers, Roger de Rabutin, Count de Bussy, commonly called Bussy Rabutin. How she could ever forgive him his offences against decency, and his slanders against herself, is one of the mysteries of the womanly heart. I never had the curiosity to read any thing of Bussy's except a few of his brevities. One does not care to plunge into dirty water; it is enough for me that Bussy shocked Louis XIV. (not an eminent model of virtue) to such a degree that the indignant monarch first put him into the Bastile, and afterwards banished him to his estates in Burgundy. Here, at Chaseux, he spent part of his seventeen years of exile; and it is one of the most extraordinary instances of the irony of fate, that the portrait of this wretched noble, who disgraced his family and his age, actually now hangs in the little village church where he heard mass, hangs over the altar, and does duty as a saint. The dress and accessories have been repainted, to suit the present destination of the work, but the worldly, seventeenth-century face looks still out of its flowing wig, between the tall candles on the altar. And the priest kneels, and the people bow, and the incense rises before it!

CHAPTER VI.

THIS etching is intended to represent one of those effects of twilight on the river which are amongst the charms of a lonely voyage. You see the great masses of the magnificent trees, but you hardly see the dark ground they stand upon, and it is not easy to tell where the water ends and the land begins. For the full enjoyment of such an hour as this, the scenery should be previously unknown to you, that the sense of mystery may be felt in its fullest intensity; but, on the other hand, there ought not to be any apprehension of danger. It is *after* a day of peril and adventure that you most enjoy the peace of the solemn gloaming, when the reaches of the river sleep in their glassy calm, and the heron lifts himself languidly on the breadth of his great gray wings.

The heron is not mentioned by accident or put in for the sake of a poetical effect. He *was* there. He passed the canoe like a winged shadow, and then rose in the calm, pure air. Just then came a great flock of rooks, and as they were flying about four hundred feet above me, the heron attained nearly the same altitude. The impertinent rooks attacked the noble bird, (fit game for peregrine falcons!) and they plagued him and insulted him till he knew not what to make of it. But he presented his sharp long beak to his assailants, and after

teasing him for a quarter of an hour they left him to take his lonely way in peace.

Danger a-head! O captain! hearest thou not the roar of the rapid?

It was time to cease gazing up into the unfathomable blue; it was time to get a firm seat and grasp the paddle well! No more enjoyment of the poetry of the twilight, only a wish for the 'light of common day,' wherein all sweet illusions fade.

It was a great rapid amongst boulders, the largest of which were as big as the room you are sitting in, dear reader. They were scattered to the right and to the left, and one or two ugly fellows apparently barred the way. The channels were narrow and deep, and the water hissed and twisted amongst them like serpents. A yellow glimmer from the evening sky shone on the swift currents, and said, 'I show you all their complexity — select!'

After another rapid, apparently much less dangerous than the first, and in reality (as often happens) much more so, the author arrived at Étang, a little old village, with two fine bridges and a railway station just built. There were some good subjects for etching in this place, especially the old houses near the river.

A relic of great interest for me (who have a peculiar weakness for tents and encamping) is preserved at the house of a rich man in the neighborhood of Étang. It is a fragment of the famous pavilion of Charles the Bold, which fell into the hands of the victorious Swiss, after the battle of Granson. The faded glory of its magnificent embroidery recalled the costliest of all the countless tents that ever trembled at the blast of trumpets, and such is the power of great associations, that the last rag and remnant of a splendor which dazzled men's eyes four hundred years ago gives poetry to the house where it is preserved, and to the very landscape that lies around it.

Étang possessed, at the time of my visit, the ugliest church (and this is saying a great deal) ever erected in the eighteenth century. Preparations were, however, being made for rebuilding it in a better form, and as the new church was to be rather larger than the old one it was necessary to make new foundations in the surrounding graveyard. This disturbed numbers of crosses which marked the graves, and these crosses were thrown all together into a corner. The graves themselves had to be cut through, and as the workmen simply dug the new foundation without troubling themselves about the bodies, they often cut them in two, so that many a dead man had his legs amputated or his head cut off in a manner quite unforeseen by his friends and relatives when they interred him near the old church wall. The writer witnessed some incidents of this kind which were not much to his taste, and when the new church stands in the glory of its Gothic arches and groined vault, and windows of brilliant stained glass, if ever he visits the place again he will never be able to see the stately walls of the fabric without thinking of the mutilated remains on each side of their deep foundations.

Two fine hills are visible from Étang, not mountains, but true hills of noble aspect with rocky heights and deep ravines. One of these is the Beuvray, mentioned in the preceding chapter as the probable site of Bibracte, and exactly opposite to the Beuvray, on the other side of the river, is the hill of Uchon, which may not have been the site of a Gaulish place of strength, but which still carries on its rocky height the tall fragment of a mediæval castle, once of considerable extent. I determined to explore this hill in detail, and gave a whole day to it, with two guides — a village schoolmaster, who kindly offered his services, and a fine boy who was one of his best scholars. The first thing to be seen was a rocking-stone, a natural curiosity of sufficiently frequent occurrence to need little description here. This stone, commonly called 'La Pierre qui croule,' or by abbreviation 'La pierre croule,' is nearly at the crest of the hill, in a large wood. Without the help of my guide I could not possibly have found it. As in the case of other rocking-stones, many attempts to remove it from its pivot have been made by stupid peasants, who have harnessed oxen to it with ropes; but the stone, which weighs nearly thirty tons, has always resisted all such attempts to deprive it of its peculiar virtue and pre-eminence. When set in motion, its movement is so regular and sure that it cracks nuts without injuring the kernel; and as the schoolmaster was provided with nuts for the occasion, and we had a boy with us willing to eat them, I had the opportunity of verifying this.

The 'Pierre qui croule' is close to a deep ravine, and near it, on the summit of the hill, were many magnificent groups of rocks. Wherever a plough could be driven, even on the very summit, the land was cultivated, and the cottages of the peasantry were scattered amongst the rocks in the little fields. The hill has an industry of its own, that of sabot-making, due to the neighborhood of the forest. I and my companions called at a cottage which was a workshop of *sabotiers*, and were very kindly received. As I was very thirsty, I begged the *sabotiers* to give me a drink of water, which one of them immediately did, in a perfectly clean but most extraordinary cup — a new sabot. I had some rum in a flask, and offered a drink to all present, on which the four workmen and three visitors provided themselves with sabots, and having half filled them with water, passed the flask to flavor it. A little incident occurred then which amused and delighted me by its quaintness and originality. It was proposed to *trinquer*, to klink,* and the seven sabots were solemnly struck against each other in token of good-fellowship. They were not the most elegant of cups, and they did not ring very musically when struck;. but after drinking out of glasses all one's life, it may be an agreeable novelty, for once, to drink out of a wooden shoe.†

Uchon is the quaintest little hill-village that I ever met with in my travels. Perched on the very highest and steepest part of the hill, not safely on the summit, but on the slope just below it, the village commands a view of immense extent. There is not a place of equal height for sixty miles before it, and the eye ranges to the illimitable plain of the Loire. It is just the site for a feudal castle, and accordingly we find the last remnant of one, a tall fragment of wall, leaning, like the Tower of Pisa, over the narrow road, with a fine Gothic fire-

---

* The old Shakespearian word.

† What added to the fun was that, in addition to the schoolmaster and boy, a friend of mine accompanied me, who is a dignitary of Autun (not mentioned in the text for that reason), and it was highly comic to see his dignity condescend to such a drinking-vessel. Some time afterwards, an old gentleman who had heard of this incident, but did not know the name of my companion, told the story, with the remark that ' no eccentricity could astonish one in an Englishman, but the wonder was how Mr. Hamerton could find a Frenchman to share his freaks.' ' That Frenchman,' replied the dignitary above mentioned, who happened to be present, ' was myself.'

place high up its side where the floor once was, and where the lady sat in her lofty chamber, and looked out on the world below. The most curious thing at Uchon is the church, which simply follows the slope of the ground, the floor in the interior being as steep as the hill-side on which the edifice is built. As the altar is at the higher end, the effect produced is really fine, and might be worth imitating artificially.

The walk was enlivened by a continual conversation with the schoolmaster, who was even more intelligent than his usually intelligent class. Amongst other interesting things, he mentioned several words which, so far as he had been able to ascertain, were peculiar to the place. Two of these were especially interesting — the verb *douler*, to suffer (Lat. *dolere*), and the substantive *vialet*, a foot-path (diminutive of *via*).

The writer, in his descent of the mountain, was in that state of excitement peculiar to landscape-painters when they find themselves in a place full of good material for study. The foregrounds were excellent, especially the magnificent old trees, and the groups of oxen and peasants in the steep little fields composed in a charmingly accidental way. The worst of it was, that, being anxious to resume my voyage, I had not time to etch upon the mountain, and the next etching I did was at noon on the following day, when I had landed in a quiet place for lunch, and the canoe lay idly on the water.

CHAPTER VII.

THE river now flowed through very majestic sylvan scenery, equal in some places to the finest parts of the Thames, and curiously destitute of every thing that we in England are accustomed to consider especially French in character. The banks were often rocky, and the foregrounds rich in heather and fern, with immense quantities of broom. Out of this rose gigantic oaks, that would have done credit to any park in England. Here is a sketch of the trunk of one which I found to be fifty feet in circumference.

This noble tree was in every respect one of the most perfectly and equally developed I ever met with. Sufficiently isolated for its growth not to be in the least interfered with, and yet at the same time not too much exposed to any prevailing wind, its massive column rose straight upwards, and its enormous branches (themselves equal to considerable trees) spread equally in every direction. I have only given the trunk here, because the attempt to represent the whole tree always failed to give any notion of its vast dimensions. Its crown of foliage, too perfect and too regular to be picturesque, was like a sylvan world erected on a pedestal. At some distance the tree did not strike one as being particularly big, probably on account of its beautiful proportions, and the not inconsiderable size of its neighbors; but

once under the shade of the great branches, the spectator suddenly becomes aware of the weight and size of the enormous limbs, and then makes deductions concerning the strength of the trunk that can support them. The impression is completed by making the tour of the trunk. The whole tree is perfectly sound, and neither lightning nor human hand has ever lopped off one branch.

An impression prevails in England that the French are indifferent to sylvan beauty, probably because wood is their principal fuel, and therefore an immense destruction of young trees takes place yearly in the forests, whilst the peasants amputate the arms of the older ones. They often, however, preserve fine timber for ornament as we do, and I learned without surprise that the fine oaks of which the giant just described was the chief and king, enjoyed, in consequence of a decree of the owner of the soil, absolute immunity from the axe. Many trees in the same neighborhood, especially the old chestnuts, must count their age by centuries, and the beeches that crest the Beuvray, though not finely developed, owing to the altitude of their situation, give every evidence of antiquity. The park of Monjeu, an estate belonging to the Talleyrand family, near Autun, is full of magnificent timber even yet, though much was destroyed by the imprudence of a man of business, who, in the owner's absence, sold it to a contractor. The haste with which this unfortunate contract was annulled, at a heavy loss, so soon as M. de Talleyrand became aware of what had been done, is a proof that he valued the timber for something more than its mere salableness. But the best evidence that the French are not indifferent to the beauty of their trees is, that scarcely a single town, however insignificant, is without its public avenues, in which the trees are encouraged to attain their fullest possible development. What English town, of equal population, has any thing comparable to the magnificent avenues that encircle Sens?

The navigation during this part of the voyage was more agreeable to the traveller himself than likely to prove interesting when narrated. Here and there the rocky bed of the stream produced narrow passes of a trifling degree of difficulty, and after them the river widened into long and tranquil reaches, over which drooped the heavy-leaved branches, dipping their extremities in the deep water that reflected them. At length, when these were gilded by the refulgence of sunset, the sound of a mill-wheel became audible in the distance, and that pleasant rush of water that may indicate either a rapid or a weir. Then a village church came into sight, and finally a few roofs of picturesque mossy thatch, which turned out to be the whole village.

The church was one of those simple old Romanesque edifices which abound in this part of France. The architects of to-day have broken with the Romanesque tradition, and in order to get more imposing effects of height and size, have adopted a very plain kind of lancet-gothic. But for a little village church I think nothing can be so well adapted as the Romanesque, with its tiny apse and aisles, and its general air of snugness, completion, and solidity on a most unpretendingly small scale. A little Romanesque church never seems to need any thing more; but a very plain, tall, lanky, modern, gothic church, with its invariable gawky tower at the west end looks hungry and uncomfortable, as if the architect had been pinched in his financial conditions, which he very generally is, and at the same time obliged

to give as many square yards of wall as possible for the money.*

The church of this little village of St. Nizier had been closed at the Revolution and never opened since. The inside was full of straw, and my canine companion rolled his wet hide upon it in a manner which appeared to indicate that he would consider it very eligible bedding if we stayed all night there. Seeing no sign of any thing like an inn amongst the half-dozen cottages which constituted the whole burgh, I felt greatly inclined to accept the dog's suggestion; but although the church was an ample and sufficiently comfortable bedroom, one could not hope to find any dinner there, and I looked about the small cottages if haply there might dwell therein some man or woman skilled in the preparation of food. Now a certain observant villager, seeing me thus in quest of something which I had not found, came with much courtesy and proffered me his services; and it turned out that this villager was in a position to be particularly useful to a traveller, for he was at the same time innkeeper and mayor, a man capable at once of nourishing the stranger, and casting over him the ægis of political protection. He lived in a small cottage whose worst defect, in my view, was that of being alarmingly damp. It had been submerged in a great flood which had happened a few weeks before, and the walls were still full of moisture that oozed out from the plaster on

---

* One of these churches was erected lately in a certain commune, and when the plans had been made I asked the priest what sort of architecture had been determined upon; but neither the priest, nor the *maire*, nor any other notable of the place, could tell me, the fact being that, though the plans had been presented for their august approval and honored therewith, they did not know the difference between one sort of architecture and another.

every side. However, here I stayed two nights, and contended against the damp by means of a blazing fire and warm bedding. The place was rather amusing, for the inn was at the same time the village shop, and my bed was in the shop itself, so I had ample opportunities for studying the inhabitants of the place. As all the villagers went to bed about sunset they did not disturb my privacy in the evening; but they began their shopping at such an uncommonly early hour in the morning that it was rather a perplexing matter how and when to go through the business of dressing. The most amusing plan seemed to be to lie quietly in bed and watch them, but this, though agreeable to a sluggardly mind, did not especially advance my own projects. One thing struck me very much, and that was the total absence of any visible stock-in-trade, yet notwithstanding this apparent deficiency every article in demand always came forth at once.

The innkeeper was a man of some culture, and both could and did read, which is more than can be said of most French villagers of his class. I found books in his house which interested me exceedingly, especially 'Charton's History of France,' which is carefully illustrated from authentic memorials of preceding centuries, not with fancy compositions invented by some artist of our own. My host was doing what he could to increase the free library in the village, already considerable enough to be a great treasury for a poor student. He took me to see it, and I certainly had not expected to find a library in a place where there was not a tiled roof, nor even a priest.

Every one who has travelled (unless he be a downright gourmand) will probably have remarked, that it is

An Etcher's Voyage of Discovery. 41

not the places where we have fared most luxuriously which usually leave the most agreeable impression upon the mind. At the fine places, we expect too much, I think, and are almost always either disappointed or within a very little of being so. I have heard a whole carriage full of men do nothing but grumble and swear as they drove home after a most extravagant Greenwich feast, and I have seen the same men quite happy and contented with a slice of beef and potatoes. In this latter frame of mind, which expects nothing, and is always satisfied with what fortune sends, did the present writer stay his two nights at St. Nizier, and he left it with a pleasing impression, as he walked down, paddle in hand, towards the rocky shore, his canoe being borne with great ceremony behind him by the mayor himself and one of the most active and influential members of the Common Council. Nevertheless, it may be acknowledged that the beautiful scenery lower down the river was not a whit the less attractive for the fact, that a renowned French cook kept an hotel somewhere in those more favored regions, an hotel where a man might not only eat, but *dine*.

CHAPTER VIII.

AFTER St. Nizier the river became even more picturesque as it proceeded. Rushing swiftly and merrily between willowy islets it carried the traveller along with very little consideration for his private tastes and preferences. The only possible exercise of choice was at the moment of selecting the channel; after that, retreat was simply out of the question, and all that could be done was to keep as clear of accident as might be. A river voyage has been compared over and over again to the course of human life, and no wonder, for the simile holds good in the minutest details, especially in such a voyage as this. How very important, for example, and, at the same time, how very difficult, it is to choose the right channel when several lie before you of which you are about equally ignorant! If you have made a mistake, if you have chosen the wrong profession or the wrong wife, then there is nothing for it but to try to get along as safely and creditably as you can, and avoid an upset if possible. If the mistake has been made it cannot be unmade, but skill and courage may still often save a man from its most disagreeable consequences. There are lives which must be as easy as it would be to paddle down the broad Loire with the ordnance map in your pocket, which shows the safest way everywhere; but these existences lose in interest what they gain in

safety, and the most interesting life to live, like the best river to explore, is one in which the course is not known in detail beforehand, but constantly calls for the exercise of skill and judgment, and is even to some degree affected also by pure hazard.

The tiny hamlets on the shores of the river were often very beautiful in their way, or, at least, very picturesque, and quite unspoiled by any modern perfections, and regularities of brickwork or of roof. Many of the best of these hamlets are of great antiquity. I know one where the cottages have not received any important addition, and have not been repaired in any other sense than that of simply replacing parts as they decayed, for the last four or five hundred years. And the life in them has followed the same unswerving tradition. The language, the religion, the customs of the inhabitants, remain almost precisely what they were in the Middle Ages. The oxen are yoked to the *char* as they were centuries ago, the *char* itself is a precise copy of that used by remote ancestors; the ploughs and other implements of agriculture are untouched by modern improvement. We know little of the lives that are led in these out-of-the-way cottages and hamlets, because it is so difficult for us to get rid of London and Paris, of literature and science, and modern thought and reflection; so difficult to realize what a life must be which neither London nor Paris influence in any perceptible way whatever, a life quite beyond the range of literature, inaccessible even to the cheapest of cheap newspapers, ignorant of every thing which makes us men of the nineteenth century instead of the fifteenth or the tenth. This simple patriarchal existence will not, however, endure very much longer; the light of modernism is breaking in upon it already here and there, through chinks in its ancient walls. It is difficult to find a place which is forty miles from a railway, and the railway brings its influences with it. A youth leaves the parental cottage for some distant place, and when he comes back gives his parents some rude notions of geography. The region through which flows 'the Unknown River' is so near to the Alps that their white crests may be seen occasionally from the summits of these hills, yet the peasants are not aware that the Alps exist. Once, however, a young man went to work at Grenoble, and he came back and told the people in his village that there were high mountains on which the snow never melted, even in the heats of summer. This is the way a little knowledge comes to them; it comes personally, by oral communication, not by books. A soldier comes back from Mexico, and tells them that Mexico is beyond the sea. I was greatly astonished at the little hamlet, here faithfully represented, to hear a man of saddened aspect speak of Boston. 'What Boston?' I asked, wondering how he should know of any Boston unless there were such a place quite near to him in France. 'It is of Boston in the United States of America, that I am speaking, sir,' answered the man of the sad countenance, astonishing me more and more, for what French peasant knows that the United States exist, or the Atlantic Ocean either? So then he told me his tale, and as it is both a pretty tale and a true one, I repeat it here for the reader.

It is simple and short enough. He and his wife were very poor indeed, almost destitute, and so, though they loved each other much, she went out as a nurse to Paris. In Paris she entered the service of some rich Americans, who, when they returned to their own country, offered her terms so tempting that she crossed the Atlantic with

them. Year after year she sent her earnings to her husband, and year after year he laid by the hard-won gold until there was enough of it to buy the cottage he lived in, and a little field or two, enough to keep them in independence all their lives. He took me into the cottage, and showed me his wife's portrait (blessings on photography, that enables a poor man to have a portrait of the absent or the dead!) and kissed it tenderly in my presence, and said how hard the long separation was, and how he looked for her return. As he said this the tears ran down his cheeks, and he showed me the bright good walnut furniture in the cottage, and the fields by the river side, and said that all this comfort was *her* doing, all this wealth *her* winning. She had learned to write on purpose that she might write to him, and month after month her kindly letters came, cheering him under the long trial of her absence. It was four years since she had left the cottage, and for these four lonely years the father had been like a widower, and the children had grown around him. And now the months went ever more and more slowly, as it seemed, when he wanted them to go faster, for this very autumn she was to sail and come to enjoy the peace she had created. May the ship that brings her paddle prosperously across the wide Atlantic, and the good woman find her way in safety to her own cottage, and to the loyal heart that yearns and waits for her so wearily!

> 'Fair stands her cottage in its place
>   Where yon broad water sweetly, slowly glides;
> It sees itself from thatch to base
>   Dream in the sliding tides.'

The character of the river became more and more strikingly picturesque as it advanced towards the Loire.

Promontories of rock jutted into the stream, which took sharp curves under steep and richly wooded banks, and went to sleep in out-of-the-way corners, where it made wonderfully perfect and tranquil harbors for the canoe. Sometimes there would be a ruin on some height, which though on a small scale, was not without grandeur, and afterwards the rich meadows and woods descended to the level of the water. Then came a long decline where the water rushed over a thousand dangerous crests of rock, and after that a pool so long and sleepy and quiet that it seemed as if the river had finally made up its mind not to flow any more, but to lie for ever in that place like a fish-pond. However, when it *did* awake and start again, it started with such freshness and energy that the interval of rest had evidently done it good, and it went gambolling amongst the rocks in a manner which, if not absolutely alarming to the canoist (one never confesses to feelings of serious alarm) did at least call for the best exercise of his skill.

In this manner we came to one of the very loveliest places I ever saw in the course of all my wanderings, a place where a rich avenue came down to the water's edge. I left the canoe and walked up between the stately trees. When the long avenue came to an end I found myself in a noble demesne with a little lake, and an island in the middle of it. On that island once stood a noble feudal castle, where royal guests have been entertained, and the castle lasted, in all its strength, till the last century, when a great fire gutted it from roof to basement. It would have been a noble ruin, but the Marquis, its proprietor, in sheer anger at the accident, utterly effaced every vestige of the stronghold of his ancestors, so that literally not one stone remains upon

another. An exquisite old gateway, of the loveliest Renaissance work, with sculpture as delicate as that of Melrose, has been re-erected at a little distance by the present owner, who inhabits a simple modern house. He intends to build a new castle more worthy of his ancient name; but an ancestral mansion, once destroyed, can never be replaced. Even an ancient avenue may be replaced in time; young trees will grow old, and they succeed each other naturally in generations, but the real feudal castle is one of those things that neither man nor nature restores when once it is destroyed and lost. We may build an imitation of it, but not the thing itself; the spirit that created it has departed, never to return. There was something terribly childish in the anger of that old marquis! The flames had destroyed the woodwork; and so, in a pet he finished what they could not achieve, and levelled all his towers!

CHAPTER IX.

A CERTAIN critic in the 'Athenæum' has lately accused the author of this little narrative * of 'intense egotism,' and not very long since somebody complained that he talked too much about his dog. Now, in the present chapter, if the story of the voyage is to be faithfully narrated, there ought to be a thrilling account of a perilous and extraordinary shipwreck, but if the writer is neither to talk about himself, nor his dog, nor any thing that is his, how is he to tell the tale? The truth is, that if you listen to critics you will never publish any thing. One critic dislikes the egotistic bits, another hates all landscape descriptions, another cannot endure any allusion to past history, another feels bored by any thing resembling philosophical reflection, a fifth scorns the repeater of an anecdote, and so on; till, if you try to please them all, simple abstinence from writing is the only thing possible for you. On the other hand, if you eliminate one of these elements in order to please one critic, the others immediately complain that it is wanting. It is a fact that a very eminent publisher complained to me a little while since that there was not enough about myself in a MS. I sent him, and too much about Julius Cæsar and the Gaulish system of fortification. Now it so happens that the present chapter might

* These chapters were first published in the *Portfolio, an Artistic Periodical.*

be dedicated plausibly enough to Julius Cæsar; for he crossed the Arroux at this very place in his chase after the Swiss, and no doubt it would be more modest, and more scholarly, to give a learned little dissertation on that event than an account of my own shipwreck. The only objection is, that most readers would skip the speculations about Cæsar.

It was already rather late in the evening, and I was sketching by the river-side at Laboulaye, and smoking the pipe of consolation. The high-road passes not far from the river at that place, and my dog-friend, hearing the sound of wheels, went to see what sort of a carriage was passing by. Soon after the carriage stopped, and I heard the sort of bark which a dog gives when he meets an old friend, a bark of joyous congratulation.

It was a fat doctor of my acquaintance, who was driving towards Toulon-sur-Arroux in the cool of the evening. It is his nature to be sociable, and he is a hater of solitude. He had recognized Tom at once, which is easy on account of·the dog's uncommon size and beauty, and so knew that I could not be far off. Then he admired the canoe. — Would I take a passenger? He would be delighted to go with me to Toulon if I would give him a berth. — Could he swim? — Swim! not in the least, but he would risk the adventure nevertheless. — Well, but then he would most likely be drowned. — He did not care if he were.

Solitude is very pleasant, but students of landscape get rather too much of it perhaps, and at times one will incur a risk for the pleasure of a genial companion. So it was settled that the doctor should send his servant on to Toulon with his carriage, and that we should see how the canoe would behave with both of us. Amongst my stores I had a waistcoat containing india-rubber airbags, to be worn whilst descending particularly dangerous rapids; so I made the doctor put this waistcoat on, and inflated the air-bags, till he looked like a pouter pigeon. All being ready, we got into our places very steadily, sitting face to face, and I took the paddle, making my passenger promise to turn neither to the right hand nor to the left. He quietly lit a cigar, and sat as coolly as if he had been on a safe ship and a deep and tranquil sea.

The river here was a series of rapids and deep pools, where the swirling water was always trying to get you under the steep walls of rock. It was necessary in several places to cross a rapid to avoid being caught between great boulders, and we had very near shaves for it once or twice. The coolness of the doctor all this time was admirable to behold. He smoked his cigar quietly and sat with perfect equilibrium, so that I had no trouble with him of any kind except for his weight, which was considerable indeed. I praised his self-possession, and he answered that he had perfect confidence in my skill. I said I could not promise to get us through such a succession of dangers without an accident. 'In that case,' he replied, 'I am satisfied that you will do what can be done, and am content to take the consequences.' 'But if we capsize you may be drowned in spite of the waistcoat — the current is tremendous.' 'I'm not afraid of death,' he answered, with unfeigned courage.

He had hardly spoken the words, when, in attempting to cross the rapid to avoid an ugly piece of polished granite, about the shape and color of a whitened skull, I found it could not be done without uncommon effort,

An Etcher's Voyage of Discovery. 51

and broke the paddle in trying. Of course, after that, the upset was inevitable. The doctor did not stir, but smoked tranquilly still, not uttering a single word; the canoe was carried against the granite, broadside on. She rose upon it a foot or two, then slipped to the right a little, the stern dipped, the water clasped me round the waist and filled the well, and she (slowly as it seemed) capsized. Just as she went over, but not before, I saw the doctor throw away his cigar. Once in the water, I found myself hurried along irresistibly, but soon got my head clear, and hoped, by surface swimming, to escape contusions on the knees. In this way I got down the rapid quite safely, and was hurled at last into a deep pool, where, after the first plunge, I felt comparatively at ease. Finding it impossible to land on the rocky side, I allowed myself to float into an eddy and was quietly carried out of the central current into a sort of tiny haven or bay, where I landed.

It then became necessary to think about the doctor. He was not far behind. Like myself, he had been carried down the rapid, and was now bobbing about in the great pool, thanks to the inflated waistcoat. But he had not the slightest notion about directing himself, and had got into a *cercle vicieux*, in a whirlpool that turned him round and round. Seeing that he would probably be carried out of the pool into some other rapid, I thought it time to set about saving him, and called out that he was not to grasp me, but simply lay his hands on my shoulders. When I approached him in the water (rather cautiously at first) he behaved with the same coolness he had displayed in the canoe. He laid a hand on each shoulder so lightly that I hardly felt it, and I towed him easily into port.

He began by expressing polite regrets, but these were interrupted by the arrival of the canoe, bottom upwards, and many articles that had been in her. There was the box of etchings, which I swam for first, and many another thing. Luckily I secured the canteen, and the doctor prescribed brandy for both of us. After that we hauled the canoe under the copse, and left it.

After walking about half an hour through a dense wood and over very rough and broken ground, we came to the river again, where it spread itself into a little lake, and at the lower end of the lake there was a weir and a mill. We looked miserable creatures, both of us. We had lost our hats, and the miller's wife took us for beggars. But the doctor entered exactly as if the place belonged to him, and declared that we must have a change of raiment. Now, considering that we were constructed by nature on totally opposite principles, resembling each other as the Tower of London resembles the Clock-tower at Westminster, it is obvious that the miller's clothes could not fit both of us. When we were dressed in this disguise, the doctor filled the miller's suit to overflowing, and looked like an over-packed carpet-bag, whereas the present writer had the appearance of a village school-boy who had suddenly outgrown his habiliments. At first the miller's wife viewed us with suspicion, but the doctor made himself so agreeable that the cloud disappeared from her countenance, and the light of it beamed upon us kindly.

By this time it was dark, and our hostess took clean, coarse sheets out of her polished presses, and laid them on two of the four beds that were in the room. But the doctor wrote a few words on a slip of paper, and sent it to Toulon by a little boy, and in a while his carriage

An Etcher's Voyage of Discovery. 53

came up to the mill with the boy in it, and under cover of night we made our entry into the town, still in our borrowed clothes. The worthy innkeeper was just going to bed when we arrived, but the active little *marmitons*, in their white jackets and caps, set to work with alacrity at their tiny charcoal fires and shining copperpans. And we sat down, in our queer costume, to the best of suppers, with wonderful appetites and joyous laughter. And so pleasantly ended our shipwreck; but it might have ended not so pleasantly as that. One thing is certain, without the inflatable waistcoat the doctor's patients would have benefited by his advice no more.

As this chapter has been written from the beginning in open defiance of criticism, I may as well sin to the very end, and speak of the faithful hound that followed me. He needed no inflatable waistcoat, but came dancing down the rapids like a cork, and never left us. He is the most indefatigable of swimmers; mile after mile did he follow the canoe, like some tame, affectionate seal. And is he not to be mentioned, — he, the unwearied follower, the brave defender, the faithful companion and friend? No one dare approach the canoe when he is there; and shall he not sup with us after our shipwreck, and be honorably mentioned here?

Ce qu'il y a de meilleur dans l'homme, c'est le chien.

CHAPTER X.

THIS little etching gives a tolerably good notion of the present condition of those fortifications which, in the middle ages, were the citadel of Toulon-sur-Arroux. The etching was made some time since; had it been executed during the last few weeks, I should have run considerable risk of being ill-used as a Prussian spy. For it is not safe, in this month of September, 1870, to draw so much as the wicket-gate of a cottage garden anywhere in France, whether you are a Frenchman or a foreigner; and if the latter, your chances are so much the worse. It had formed part of my plan to republish this series of papers with additional etchings on a larger scale, and I began these additional plates in the month of July, intending to revisit the scenery of the whole river, and select about a dozen of the finest subjects. I had done a few of these when the great spy mania took possession of all French minds, at least in the lower classes, and there arose such a hubbub about my doings over an extent of country thirty miles in diameter, that it would have been absolute madness to let myself be seen with any thing of the nature of drawing materials about me. So the larger etchings were brought to an abrupt termination. The reader, who is by this time familiar with the slight and purely artistic little plates which have illustrated these chapters, will be amused at the notion

that they can be supposed to be of any imaginable utility to Von Moltke and the Crown Prince in their brilliant invasion of France; but the peasantry in these parts have made up their ingenious minds on the subject, and as to arguing with them, one might as well try to argue with a tribe of hostile savages. Like the country people in England, they confound drawing with surveying, and believe that artists are men employed to make maps. Who employs them? that is the next question; and the answer, of course, is, 'The King of Prussia.'* When I made these little plates at Toulon, I was enjoying one of the blessings and privileges of peace. He would be a bold man to-day, who would sit down and draw a citadel anywhere in France, even though it had been dismantled for the last three hundred years.

Here, again, is the bridge. If any one drew that bridge to-day, it would clearly be that the Prussians might pass over it. But in those happy times of peace, the peasants felt rather flattered that a 'map' should be made of their bridge, and the more knowing ones suggested that, since the present writer made such good maps of bridges, he would do well to make one of the new railway-bridge at Étang, which was of iron, and perfectly straight, and had been pushed from shore to shore all in a single piece, just as you would put a plank over a rivulet.

Toulon is a very quaint little town, with a rather picturesque market-place on a hill-top, and the streets slop-

* In the good old times, before Bismarck was heard of, *travailler pour le roi de Prusse* used to mean working without any probability of payment. In that sense, undoubtedly, the present writer, like most artists, has worked a good deal for the King of Prussia. But tell it not in Gath, repeat it not in the villages of Burgundy! a pleasantry of that kind, in these times, might cost the jester's life.

ing down on all sides to the river and the surrounding country. On the top of the hill is the old citadel, of which one tower serves for the tower of the old church. The population of Toulon has diminished of late years, but the church, which used to be considered quite large enough for the place (a quaint old Norman-looking edifice), has not satisfied the ambition of the present incumbent, who saw big churches rising in all the neighboring villages, and thought he might as well have a big church too. So he raised a subscription and built one, but a certain pillar of it was unfortunately erected immediately over an old well, and the covering of the well gave way, and the pillar went down into it, as a steel ramrod used to go down the barrel of a rifle before these breech-loading times.

In lonely travel the great secret of avoiding *ennui* is to take an interest in the people as well as the scenery. Any one who is on the look-out for characters is always sure to meet with them. For instance, I found a doctor at Toulon who smoked without ceasing when he was awake, except when he laid down his pipe to take his knife and fork. He was an old man, in perfect health, and still in full professional practice. This last fact may seem incompatible with incessant smoking, and would, no doubt, be so in London; but in a tiny town where everybody knew the doctor, he was indulged in his habit by everybody. I spent a good many hours with him, and during the whole time he was doing one of two things, either smoking his pipe or filling it. He had read most of our best authors in the original, having taught himself English alone, with the help of nothing but books. He had a capital little English library at home, and had read every volume in it: all Scott, all

Dickens, all Shakespeare, Byron, and many others. His pronunciation was, of course, as bad as our pronunciation of Latin; and I felt on hearing him read a little, as an old Roman would feel if he could go to Oxford and hear the men there deliver Latin orations. However, in this instance, there was nothing to laugh at, because there was no pretension, and the doctor knew our literature better than many Englishmen do, and understood it, and loved it. He had never heard an English word pronounced by a native before he hit upon me, so that I was a real *trouvaille;* and he was extremely kind to me, and invited me to breakfast, pointing out a charming harbor for the canoe at the end of his garden, as a temptation to future voyages.

But the best character in Toulon was the *maire* of the place, Monsieur B., an artist of reputation in a much more useful line than any etcher. I fear that no plate of mine will ever give Monsieur B. half as much pleasure and satisfaction as the *plats* of his cooking gave to me. He keeps the hôtel where I stayed, and he made me a little portable *déjcûner* to take with me every morning when I set out to work. French cookery is always either exquisite or abominable, and his was of the former. Monsieur B. is a very celebrated man indeed. People write from a distance to order a dinner, and then travel to Toulon to eat it. Unfortunately, he is also celebrated as the most irascible man in the country; which, considering the generally explosive character of French tempers, is saying a good deal. As that man must be a wonderfully perfect Sabbatarian who can win fame in Scotland for his observance of the day of rest, so that Frenchman must be irascible indeed who can make himself famous for his irritability. His powers of voluble invective surpassed all that I had ever heard in the way of scolding, and their effect was immensely enhanced by the most scientific modulation of tone. His loud voice disturbed me in the early morning as he scolded a boy-cook for having used a pound of first-rate butter, reserved especially for pastry, in cooking yesterday's dinner. Now the misapplication of the butter was commented upon in a restrained and subdued *piano*, with deep concentrated rage, and now it passed with a rapid crescendo to *forte* and a terrible *fortissimo*, that made the very windows rattle. When a servant is to be reprimanded, the first observations are made in the utmost moderation, and if only Monsieur B. could stop there, he would deserve the credit of being a reasonable though vigilant master; but the sound of his own voice exasperates him, and even when the culprit offers no reply, his fault is described to him over and over again, every time with increasing vehemence, till at length the floodgates of invective are opened wide and the torrent rolls and roars.

Yet nothing can exceed Monsieur B.'s politeness to his guests. In the midst of his loudest furies, he will turn aside and speak to you with a serene countenance and gentle voice, whilst over the door of the dining-room is the inscription : —

'*Rien ne doit déranger l'honnête homme qui dîne.*'

CHAPTER XI.

THE admirers of beautiful scenery are often somewhat narrow, and even bigoted, in their admiration. It has been the fashion, for the last half-century, to enjoy mountain scenery very much, and to undertake long journeys in search of it; but the proof that this love of nature is rather the love of a certain kind of exhilaration, to be had best in mountainous districts, is that most people still remain perfectly indifferent to the beauty of the plains. They can understand that you have reasonable motives for going to Switzerland or the Tyrol, but what can you see to care for on the Loire? 'Mere poplars, you know, and that sort of thing,' say the few who have visited the river that Turner loved. Therefore I feel a little apprehensive that the sympathy of many readers, which has gone with me whilst I had to speak of rocks and rapids, and heathery hills purple in the evening, may leave me now that I come to the broader waters and less romantic landscapes of the plain.

And yet, when the last rapid had been passed, and the river spread into sleepy reaches, only occasionally interrupted by the gentle murmur of a safe and sandy shallow, over which the canoe glided like a boat on some languid stream; when the sun at evening, instead of suddenly and prematurely disappearing behind the wooded heights, sank slowly in the immensity of the clear heaven, till he set on the far horizon as he sets on the summer sea, there came upon the spirit of the voyager such a sense of boundless space, and free breathing of balmy illimitable air, as he never knew in the narrow gorges where dark hills and dense woods overshadowed him.

Every scene of nature has its own character, and its own charm. The plains have not the sublimities of the hills, nor the guarded seclusion of the shaded valleys, and we miss the weird shapes of the gray rocks that breast the stream where its flowing is strongest; yet it is glorious to see all the blue sky in the daytime, and all the stars at night. And the river seems to gain a certain dignity too, with its assurance of perfect peace. It has space for all its waters, and knows restraint no more. The graceful trees only adorn its borders, but do not arrest its course. If it winds in beautiful curves, it does so from deliberate preferences. It would be easy, as it seems, to go straight to its distant bourn, but to go indirectly is yet a little easier; so it turns for its own pleasure, and visits here a village, and there a solitary farm, where the oxen stand knee-deep in the evening.

The gradual growth of a river might be illustrated by drawings of its bridges. First you have the trunk of a single tree, rudely flattened on the upper side by strokes of a peasant's axe, and supported by two rude abutments of unhewn granite blocks. A little lower down the stream has become too wide for the single trunk to cross it; so now you have two trees that meet on a rock in the middle. After that you come to the first serious attempt at construction : a wooden bridge for foot-passengers only, the cattle and cart traffic still passing through the water in a shallow ford a little below; then

An Etcher's Voyage of Discovery. 61

comes the first stone bridge, a single arch, if the people are rich enough to afford a piece of accomplished engineering, but, if the village masons have done the work, more usually two or three tiny arches, that a stray cow might possibly pass under, and which are pretty sure to be choked with water in a flood which will wash over the rude parapet. As the river widens it passes near some town or city, and then we find the stately stone bridge of careful masonry — three arches, perhaps — where the high-road enters the town. After that the number of arches increases, till at last you meet with those long and stately constructions, whose fine perspective attracted Turner so much when he illustrated the rivers of France.

The accompanying sketch, which represents the bridge of Gueugnon, gives evidence that the Unknown River has quite grown out of the romantic and tumultuous period of its existence, and become a sober stream capable even of rendering service to navigation, if it were worth while to deepen a few shallows here and there. Indeed, from this bridge to the Loire the river is classed amongst those which, if not positively navigable, might easily be made so.

Gueugnon is rather an industrial place, as may be guessed from the smoky chimneys in the etching, which belong to some ironworks, where they make wire, and sheet-iron for tinning. Here the traveller found an iron canoe, flat-bottomed, and extremely even uncomfortably narrow. She must have been terribly crank; but that is a defect the body accustoms itself to so easily that, after a fortnight's practice, one sits in a crank boat as easily as in a stiff one. There is usually a certain amount of jealousy amongst boat-builders, and the mechanic who had made the iron canoe spoke very disparagingly of mine, which I took with British coolness, merely inquiring whether he had ever descended the rapids in his invention, which was entirely without a deck, and would have certainly gone to the bottom like a lump of lead after half a dozen waves had washed into it. The crowd around us seemed to consider that the best proof of the quality of my own vessel was her successful voyage down the wildest parts of the river. After that, the inimical mechanic became suddenly very amiable, and conducted me over the ironworks, explaining every process most politely. The reason for this amiability became evident at last; for just as I left him, and thanked him, he proposed to build me an iron canoe which should be made exactly according to my own fancy, and have a deck, and every thing I had a mind to. In a word he was a shipbuilder (on a very small scale) touting for orders. Had the present writer been a permanent resident at Gueugnon, it would have been rather a tempting proposal, as there is no employment in the world more congenial to his feelings than superintending the construction of a boat.

There is a great weir at Gueugnon, which offers a slope of most excellent masonry very like a great railway embankment, and when the water flows over it, in one smooth sheet, it would be delightful to glide down it in a canoe. Unfortunately, however, there are rude stones at the bottom, which would give the adventurer a most unpleasant reception. I got amongst these stones in the dark, and had plenty of trouble with them — the last inconvenience of that kind in the course of the voyage.

There was a comfortable inn at Gueugnon — well,

An Etcher's Voyage of Discovery. 63

comfortable is perhaps hardly the word for any French inn of that class, but these things go by comparison, and, after lodging in peasants' cottages amongst the hills, it seemed quite stately and luxurious to sit at dinner in the evening with two candles in tall candle-sticks on the table, and an attentive waiter at one's elbow.

The etching opposite shows the way in which I used to have to seek for a lodging when belated, and it was always disagreeable to me, mainly on account of the necessary, yet almost impossible explanations. How can you make a peasant understand your purposes in an artistic excursion of any kind? How, especially, can you make him understand such purposes when complicated with the amusement of canoing?

On a fine night it was positively more agreeable to sleep in the canoe, in the manner represented at the close of the chapter. Since then the author has invented much more luxurious arrangements;* but it was not unpleasant to make a bed of rushes, and sleep soundly and softly, covered up to the chin with waterproofs to guard one from the dews of the night. Many a poor

* This alludes to a contrivance by which a hut and a punt are united in one construction. During the day, the punt, which is of wood, contains a second punt of tinned iron. The iron punt is divided into several compartments, in the largest of which sits the canoist. All the other compartments are closed. Two of them are kept accessible by movable lids; one of these is used for provisions and the other for clothing. That for provisions contains eight boxes fitted to each other carefully, in which may be kept the different requisites for a week's voyage, and a complete cooking apparatus. That for clothing contains a change of dry clothes, a hammock, &c., and bedding. When night comes the boat is drawn up on the shore, and the tin punt removed from the interior of the wooden one. Two light frames are then fixed upright in the wooden punt, and the tin one is easily lifted upon these frames. A double curtain is then fixed all round, and we have a hut with a wooden floor, a metallic roof, and canvas sides. In this hut the hammock is easily suspended.

soldier in the present war, forced to lie on the bare ground, often stony and muddy, would consider these contrivances a luxury. It was something, too, before going to sleep, to look up at the moonlit clouds and the stars in the depths between them.

This contrivance has been completely realized in every detail, but I have never had an opportunity of using it, because, during the summer of 1870 there was no water in the rivers, and since the beginning of the Prussian War it would be madness to show one's self in any such mysterious-looking invention, as it would set all the peasants perfectly mad. In times of sanity and peace it seems to me that nothing could be better adapted for a tour such as that described in these pages. It is unpleasant to have to leave work undone in order to go five or six miles lower down a river to seek for a lodging. Many etchings were left unfinished for that reason in the excursion here narrated, and have consequently been thrown aside. Many subjects remarkably suited for etching had also to be passed without illustration when the weather was not mild enough for a bivouac.

CHAPTER XII.

ON leaving Gueugnon, in the cool of a bright autumn evening I saw a magnificent piece of black oak which had been disengaged from the bed of the river during the great inundation, and thrown upon the high shore. The whole trunk was complete, and measured seventy feet in length by forty in girth. I cut it in several places with a penknife and found it as black as ebony. How many centuries it had lain in the river's bed I know not, but, judging from the color and condition of the wood, which was all black bog-oak of the finest quality, the tree must have lain beneath the flowing water as long as the black oak in the deepest bogs of Ireland. What noble chambers might have been furnished out of it! what rich inlaying of parquets and wainscot would it not have supplied!

The landscape now began to wear an aspect of uncommon sadness and desolation. The river divided itself into many straggling currents in a wide desert of sand and pebbles. A low, yellow precipice of the same material hid all the fields from my sight, as I sat low in the canoe on the level of the dreary gray water. How mournfully, too, the water seemed to murmur down its tortuous, divided channels! For miles and miles there was nothing to be seen except a great château on the top of a bare slope, a long, ugly, melancholy building, enough to make one miserable to look at it, and think that any one could be condemned to live in it.

When I came near this château, the twilight was already very far advanced, and I landed to eat a little supper. The land was bare of trees, a desolate expanse of uncultivated soil, where a herd grazed in the distance. Suddenly I wondered not to see Tom galloping towards me, as he generally had done at these improvised mealtimes on the shore. I called and whistled for him long and loudly, but in vain, and during all that remained of the voyage I saw his affectionate face no more. This caused me some anxiety, and rather spoiled my pleasure, but I trusted that he would find his way home again. On my return I made inquiries, and found that he had first returned to the inn at Gueugnon, after losing me in the tortuous channels of the river, and stayed at the inn till *déjeûner* the next morning. After his meal he suddenly disappeared, and the innkeeper could give no further account of him. The same evening, however, he arrived at my house, a distance of fifty kilometres, where he rushed to his kennel at once, and fell down in it like lead, exhausted. The next day he was all right again. But it was a severe run, for no doubt he had made the fifty kilometres a hundred, and followed the river's brink in the thick underwood; often, I dare say, swimming against the stream. I never knew such a persistent swimmer. He never had the sense to follow the canoe on the bank, but would always swim behind it, however cold the water or long the distance. It was this which had separated him from me. Being rather pressed for time in the late evening, I had pushed on too fast for Tom.

An Etcher's Voyage of Discovery.   67

The voyage had been a lonely one from the beginning, but it seemed doubly solitary after the loss of my companion. I had never been able to do with him in the canoe, — he was much too large and heavy for that, — but every time I landed, either to make an etching or eat a dinner — and I never did either afloat — Tom had always joined me, and so the long solitude had been made less difficult to endure. I humbly thank Divine Providence for having invented dogs, and I regard that man with wondering pity who can lead a dogless life.

The dreary hours and the dreary landscape both came to an end at the same time. The moon rose, trees began to reappear on the river's brink, the scattered currents met together again, and there were vistas of prolonged perspective. I remember one especially, a scene of most perfect and extraordinary beauty. For a length of about a thousand fathoms the stream was straight as a cathedral aisle, and at about half the distance there was a transept on each side, that might have been designed by art. All along, the shores were shaded by the richest foliage. Boughs hung gracefully till they dipped their golden leaves in the glassy water. Tall poplars rose at intervals, like towers, to mark the far perspective. It was midnight. A pure semi-transparent mist filled the still and silent air, and above in the clear heaven shone the round and brilliant moon. Not a sound was to be heard but the alternate dip of the paddle, which I used as gently as might be, for it seemed wrong to break so beautiful a mirror. At last I toiled no more, and the little boat glided on and on with its own motion, as if drawn by invisible spirits. During the whole voyage I had found nothing so exquisite as this, nor has any other impression fixed itself so perfectly in my memory.

That scene was too ethereal to be etched, but next day I drew this bridge, partly because it was the last bridge on the Unknown River, and partly as a memorial of the great and disastrous flood. In these terrible months of 1870, when a thousand bridges that spanned the fair rivers of France, have been ruined to check the progress of an invader more to be dreaded than any inundation, men pray that the rains may fall and the waters rise till the streams are all torrents and the plains all inland seas.

After this bridge, the scenery of the shore began to assume the large aspect that belongs to the stately Loire. A steep bank rose in the distance, clothed with vines and crowned with a group of buildings clustering round convent-towers. The current became swifter, as if the Unknown River were hastening to its end; it curved rapidly once or twice, then suddenly behold an expanse of broad water before me, flowing westwards, and before I had time quite perfectly to realize the change, the canoe was carried out upon the Loire.

And so the voyage came to a successful end, and for the first time since first his waters flowed, the Unknown River has been navigated. Shall I conclude with a triumphant boast, and affirm that although Gaul and Roman have dwelt upon its shores, and reddened it in sanguinary conflict, its perfect exploration was reserved for the audacity of an Englishman? Let me rather, more modestly, rejoice in sharing that capacity for taking pleasure in the beauty of natural scenery which belongs to so many in our own time. It is this, much more than any particular satisfaction in the somewhat monotonous business of paddling, which constitutes the principal charm of all canoe voyages, and it is this,

more peculiarly and especially, which made privations light to me, and labor pleasant, and time swift, during the weeks I spent in, 'An Etcher's Voyage of Discovery.'

RESULTS.

A FEW words concerning the especial purpose of this voyage — etching from nature — may possibly be of use to a few readers who may undertake etching tours.

No art is more agreeable for direct work from nature than etching is. The rapidity of it, and its freedom, are greatly in its favor, and so is its remarkable independence of damp and wet. Many of the plates in this series were immersed in the river, after being etched, when the artist was upset; others were executed in bad weather, with the rain literally pouring over the copper in a manner which would have rendered any other kind of drawing quite impossible. In the course of the excursion I did sixty plates, from which these are selected. It is better, I think, to be rather prolific in production, and select afterwards the plates which seem most successful, than to spend much time in correcting bad plates in the studio. My advice to etchers would be to spend time rather in doing many plates than in polishing and mending a few. This may be contrary to the feeling of some painters, who rightly, in their art, obey the maxims of Boileau; but whatever value an etching may have depends mainly on the inspiration of the moment. If it were only possible to possess that inspiration always, the art would be easier than it is. The only consolation I have to suggest for the many failures and the disappointing uncertainty which ever attend it, is that it leads us to work from nature, and look at nature, in the most essentially artistic spirit.

THE END.

www.ingramcontent.com/pod-product-compliance
Lightning Source LLC
Chambersburg PA
CBHW031457160426
43195CB00010BB/1004